A PILGRIM IN ASSISI

Searching for Francis Today

Susan Saint Sing

St. Anthony Hospital

Photographs on pages iv, 6, 12, 16, 19, 26, 34, 41, 54, 62, 68, 73, 84, 86, 93, 107 by Murray Bodo.

Photographs on pages 2 and 65 by Bill Barrett.

Photographs on pages 9 and 48-49 by John Quigley.

Photographs on pages 58 and 81 by Susan Saint Sing.

Cover and book design by Julie Van Leeuwen.

SBN 0-912228-85-7

To Murray and Francis
       who were there;
  Joe and Leopold
       who believed;
  Drs. Lucas and Smith
       who encouraged;
  Sam and Thaddeus
       who shared with me their spirits;
  Don Aldo, Ave, Severina, Damien
       and all the brothers of The Group.

Foreword

You bring something with you to Assisi. Perhaps it is faith, perhaps something you have heard or something you remember rising from your soul. Perhaps it is a last desperate hope that maybe this is the end of the journey for your pilgrim heart. Why else would you stop here in this quiet, medieval town instead of going on to those two meccas of the art lover and the pilgrim, Florence to the north and Rome to the south? It is Francis, of course, who holds you here in this little town, Francis of Assisi. The name itself is enough to make even the most casual tourist pause and wonder about staying the night.

My own pilgrimage here began a long time ago when, as a boy of 13, I read a life of St. Francis in a corner of the junior high library in Gallup, New Mexico. Twenty-two years later I stepped onto the train platform of Assisi, bringing with me the realization that the journey to Assisi takes a long time because it is a journey of the soul.

Assisi for me is a town of symbols and

mystery. It belongs somehow to the olive trees, and Francis belongs to them both. He is entwined with the roots of these ancient trees and lies like mortar between the pink stones of Assisi's houses. In order to understand the radical and even somewhat terrible commitment of Francis to the crucified Christ, it is necessary to look at these old, twisted olive trees that cling tenaciously to the sides of Mount Subasio.

They are old; some say the oldest olive trees in Italy. They are rooted with a stubbornness akin to Francis' own single-willed determination to follow the Christ who spoke to him from the crucifix at San Damiano. Like these trees, Francis was immovable in his total devotion to gospel poverty—and like them he has outlasted all the years and seasons of change and progress.

And like the pink stones of Assisi he has remained attractive though architectures and styles in the Church have changed. The mortar of his spirit holds these stones together just as the real mortar he made with his own hands held together the first little churches he repaired: San Damiano, San Pietro, Santa Maria degli Angeli.

The outward configuration of trees changes, but they endure if they are rooted well. Franciscans, too, have changed in their configuration, even to some extent in their life-styles, but the roots are still there. They are found in the writings of Francis and in the spirit that breathes between his sparse and simple words. They are in the simple story of his life, and they are in Assisi itself. There is more than mystique to this town. In the geography of Assisi is the landscape of St. Francis' soul.

This book is a meditation on the spirituality of Francis from the viewpoint of the places in which it is rooted. Like the olive trees of Mount Subasio Francis is inseparable from this land, this place and space of growing. Like the stones and mortar of its houses he belongs to this town. Always he is St. Francis of *Assisi.*

Murray Bodo, O.F.M.

Contents

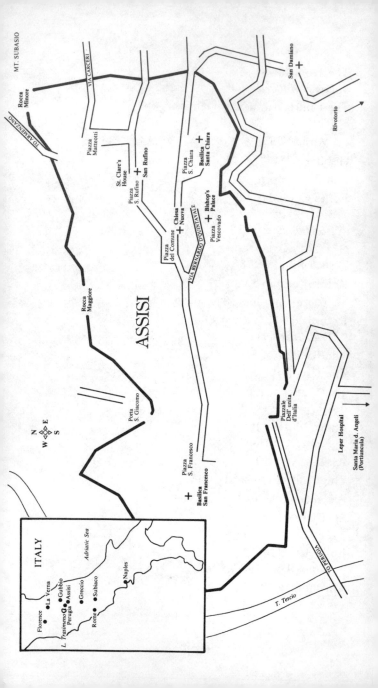

A Word From the Author

A *Pilgrim in Assisi* is a meditative celebration of the Assisi of Saint Francis, written for all the pilgrims who will visit there during the commemoration of the 800th anniversary of Francis' birth and for all of those who want to go but cannot.

My reflections as a lay Franciscan tell the story of Francis through the places of his life as I encountered them—a pilgrim walking the streets of his city, wandering over the countryside which is intimately a part of his story. The reflections follow the order of events in Francis' life, though occasionally paths cross and familiar spots are revisited. I hope my footsteps are those of any pilgrim who encounters the traces of the saint in stones and sunlight, the scent of ginestra and the weather's changing moods—as well as the inner stirrings of one's heart.

To help the armchair pilgrim who wants to identify the seasons of Francis' life, a chronology can be found on page 117.

Mount Subasio

Mount Subasio, rising 4,229 feet, shelters Assisi from the severe eastern winds. The ancient people of Umbria built their city on a small, sunny rise 1,656 feet high on Subasio's west slope. The mountain, with its deep forests and streamlets, was a favorite hermitage site for Francis and the brothers.

It is morning. As I lean out my shuttered window over Via San Paolo, I am filled with freshness. Mount Subasio lies striped with clouds as the sun begins its ritual of burning away the morning mists, revealing the farms and cottages on the plain below. Swallows soar, bells peal, pink granite warms as Assisi awakes again.

I am a pilgrim here. Among the shops filled with ceramic friars, the castle towers and the churches, I search for what I hope to find. But I am not sure it is here. Straining through the mists, I see robed brothers singing and clapping one another on the shoulders, their feet cuddling the soil on the plain below. Another wisp unfurls and I see it is only the wheat piled high to dry.

I am climbing to the top of Mt. Subasio today, high above the rattle of the streets and the stares of the shopkeepers. My little path, probably centuries old, used to lead the cattle from the stifling valley to the cool grasses on the mountaintop. I walk past Francis' cave, up through the forest of the Carceri. I use a ladder already in place to scale a barbed wire fence, and the hot mixture of wheat and wild flowers nearly suffocates me. Wind rushing up the bleached granite face is a welcome friend.

I wonder if Francis ever came to this very spot. Dangling my feet over the edge of the cliff and letting my sandals serve as a pillow, I watch a small bird sailing on the wind. My soul quietly stops its longing. Warmed by the Umbrian sun, I know I am home.

Francis' Birthplace

At the end of the street where Francis'
parents lived, there was a small stable
for their animals. According to a 15th-
century legend, when Lady Pica's hour
had come the baby could not be born.
Then a pilgrim knocked at the door and
said the child would not be born till
Lady Pica left her bedroom and went
into the stable. She lay down in one of
the stalls and bore a son whose first
cradle, like that of the Savior, was a
manger full of straw.

Out in the street little bambinos are
kicking their soccer ball against the wall of a bar.
The shopkeeper comes out and yells, raising his fist
and sounding very important as the little boys grab
their ball and run to another wall.

This is the street where Francis played
as a boy. He probably leaned against these walls at
one time or another. In this street he grew up,
playing with wooden toys his father had made for
him. Shrieks and laughter echo through the tiny
alley; the boys have found another wall. I wonder if
Francis laughed like that?

Legend says Francis' mother crossed the
stones of this alley when a pilgrim prophesied that

her baby would be born in their stable. Years later they were crossed again by an angered Pietro Bernardone, dragging his son by the scruff of his neck to Bishop Guido. And the prophecy announced at Francis' birth began to unfold in reality. This son would pattern his life after another who had also been dragged across the streets and handed over to ridicule and judgment.

Rocca Maggiore

The Rocca Maggiore was built as a Roman garrison by Barbarossa in 1174. It commands a view of Perugia to the west, south across the Umbrian plain, northward up the Tescio gorge and east to Mt. Subasio. The castle was partially destroyed in 1198 when Assisians rebelled against the Duke of Spoleto; it was later rebuilt by the Papal States. Its fortifications buffered Assisi from neighboring enemies, such as Perugia. In 1201 Francis himself was captured by the Perugians and imprisoned for a year. Today it stands as one of the most dramatic and important fortifications of medieval times.

Francis was a youth of many homes, equally at wits with the arrogant young Assisians whooping through the streets as he was pensive and serious, stealing off alone to some favorite secluded wall to sit and think. Surely Umbrian nights then were as beautiful as they are now. Did he ever sit here at the Rocca Maggiore? It gives such vantage of the road to Perugia and the plain below. Maybe he would walk away from the singing company of friends and come to this granite wall overlooking

the flickering candles of the cemetery far below, pondering Assisi's enemies' attempts to scale this cliff and capture the town.

The air is laced with ginestra and dry grass. A dog is barking in the distance and fireflies magically dance on the darkening hill. I reach down and pull a tassel off a weed and place it thoughtfully between my teeth. I meet a U.S. Army sergeant from the Yugoslav border, and we talk of his duties and expectations as Perugian lights flicker near in the west.

Suddenly a mad clanging of bells sounds a historic but unheeded curfew. Spitting out the blade of grass, I pick my way back down the veins of steps to the piazza and join some of my friends for brandy and ice cream. Amid smiles, laughter and furtive glances from promenading Italian boys, my thoughts are caught up in the gaiety of Assisi. We all excitedly exchange our tales of the day's experiences. But quiet pauses tell me that sometimes the most precious moments are too sacred to be shared, even with the dearest of friends.

Chiesa Nuova

Like many sites in Assisi, there is much controversy about whether the Chiesa Nuova is truly the site of the Bernardone household and shop. Nevertheless, the church was built in 1615 by Philip III of Spain to protect and venerate the rooms where Francis was believed to have lived and worked. Inside, directly to the left of the main entrance, is a small cell where Pietro imprisoned Francis as punishment for selling cloth to gain money for repairing the little church of San Damiano. Pietro's shop is located beneath the church; along the inside stairway is the door through which Lady Pica passed to the stable where Francis was born. In Francis' room (now the presbytery) he prophetically dreamed of the palace full of banners and shields where a Lady awaited him and his knights.

Sheets of rain are splashing down, and rippling streamlets rush along the stones. To the left the of doorway to Chiesa Nuova (New Church) is a lesser entrance more hidden and unnoticed—a perfect place to see from and not be

seen. I don't know why I am repeatedly drawn back to this street, his street, and this house, his house; maybe it is because I sense here the mundane street life and the experience of growing up that shaped Francis.

After he turned back from the army, Francis walked this street in disgrace. No longer did he lead the pranks as a proud son of Assisi. He was called a coward—and to a young man who wants to be a knight, honor is all. Francis had lost his honor and shamed the Bernardone name. He was alone. His friends were off to war or forbidden to associate with him. He was sick and weak, mentally distraught and exhausted from his dream at Spoleto. In the dream a voice had asked him, "Francis, which is it better to serve, the master or the servant?"

"The master," he replied.

"Then go and do so."

What did that mean? He returned to Assisi, spending sleepless nights and lonely days sitting here, staring blankly into the streets, clinging to the seclusion of this doorway while he waited for another word. He sat alone, waiting for some sign, some meaning to the voice and the great hall of shields.

The depths of his own spent emotions were the beginning of his great compassion. He had been weak and abandoned as he would never again let others be. He had despaired and would try to bring others hope. He had felt anger and confusion and one day, when he was well, he would bring light and peace to those around him.

Suddenly I am aware that my soggy sneakers are damming up a streamlet anxious to be on its way. Looking at my watch, I realize I have been standing here staring into this passageway for nearly an hour. Turning back to the Piazza del Comune I hear the bells from the Basilica of St. Francis ringing out. Their lively resonance echoes within me, telling me that Francis did not sit here and wait in vain.

Piazza del Comune

The Piazza del Comune, with its famous fountain, is the main town square of Assisi. Today it is flanked by the town hall, banks, the post office, colorful cafes and shops. After the battle of Sentino in 295 B.C., Assisi became a Roman municipium *with the duty of providing soldiers to the legions. The remains of this era are evident in the Temple of Minerva (now the church of Santa Maria Sopra Minerva) whose Corinthian columns rise from the north side of the piazza, in traces of Roman baths and an amphitheater. Beneath the present-day road surface of the piazza are the ruins of the Forum. Its arches, statues and reliefs witness to a once flourishing scenario. Now they stand sentinel over a part of history we can walk through but never relive.*

To Francis, friends and friendship were very special. With his father away for long periods of time on cloth-buying trips, Francis was left to run the shop, look after his mother and entertain himself. Always the center of attention, he would act out chivalric legends to the cheers of his

friends. Francis was a born actor who had heard over and over again the troubadours' tales of great heroism and knights in shining armor.

Tonight as I sit in the Piazza del Comune, bleachers are set up around a tiny stage as scenes from the *Fioretti (The Little Flowers of St. Francis)* are performed by Assisi youth.

Taxi drivers lie on their horns and stretch out of their windows to yell at other motorists—and then pull their heads inside with a smile and a shrug; it's all a performance for them. Whoever outperforms the other is considered the cleverer and more respected person.

I cannot help but wonder if at first Francis looked upon episodes like begging in borrowed rags at St. Peter's tomb in Rome as performances—performances totally for himself, but performances none the less. Even if they were performances at the beginning, with each encounter with the *real* beggars Francis was slowly caught up in the depth of pain in the eyes of his newfound friends.

And in this crust of humanity, without all the frills and flamboyant dress and conversation of his Assisi friends, Francis could see true people. Naked and dirty, ugly and diseased but sincerely and tangibly real, they were friendless except for each other and for this mysterious rich young man who repeatedly came to them to receive rather than to give.

The Bishop's Palace

*On the Piazza Vescovado is the
reconstructed Bishop's Palace. In 1206
Francis was brought before the bishop
by his father for selling Pietro's cloth to
aid repairs on San Damiano. In the
piazza before all the townspeople,
Francis renounced his father, gave him
back all his earthly possessions—even
his clothes—and announced his loyalty
to his Father in heaven. The bishop
draped his own cape around the young,
naked Francis. Twenty years later,
suffering from years of hardship, disease
and the wounds of the stigmata, Francis
was brought to Bishop Guido again to
rest and recover in the safety and peace
of the palace. But realizing his death
was imminent, he asked to be taken to
the Portiuncula, where he died.*

Here in the palace courtyard is a
statue of St. Francis. The pose of this statue always
catches me, no matter how frenzied I may be when
passing it, and pulls me into a long gaze upon its
lines. You cannot see Francis' face, for it is bowed.
And his hands are clasped gently beneath his
sleeves. He stands somewhat round-shouldered with

his feet sandaled, not bare. Many hours I have sat and stared at this form, wondering why it is so mesmerizing. Again and again I come back to it.

Finally one day I realized what it is that fascinates me: The lines of his head and upper body form a perfectly shaped inverted heart pointing upward to heaven. Once I realized what I had been seeing I was drawn to it all the more. Of course! Francis' whole life, direction and being was his love of God. Francis' heart was totally absorbed with his Lord. The artist wanted to capture and symbolize this direction using lines soft as flesh and bronze warm as an embrace from the Umbrian sun.

The statue is so public, misplaced too near the street with a ring of grass surrounding it and cars parked all around it. Yet it gives one the impression of total solitude and rapture. As I walk away I wonder if I have projected too much into a simple piece of sculpture. But then I think of Francis, standing in the public streets, and I feel certain the artist wanted me to stop and take a long look and walk away thinking of the direction of my own heart.

San Damiano

*This was the church which Francis
restored in 1205 when the crucifix
miraculously spoke to him. It was the
first cloister of the Poor Clares and
where Francis came in his illness to be
cared for by Clare. Here he wrote the
Canticle of Brother Sun. At his death
his body was passed through the small
window in the apse to be reverenced by
Clare and her sisters one final time.
Clare died here in 1253. Her body was
later removed to her Basilica and a new
cloister built in her honor within Assisi's
walls. Today San Damiano is occupied
by the friars and remains much as it was
in the time of Francis and Clare.*

I love to come here, especially in the
afternoon when the tourists and Assisians are
taking a siesta. In the darkness of this last pew I
can touch the damp stones and murmur, "Brother
Rock." Here, cradled by their strength and shelter,
Francis becomes present to me, and I finally
understand what Jesus meant when he said, "...the
very stones would cry out" (Luke 19:40). The cross
that spoke to Francis isn't here anymore. For its
protection it was given to the Poor Clares, and it

hangs today at the Basilica of St. Clare.

It was at his Baptism, amidst all the splendor and wealth of the Cathedral of San Rufino, that Francis received the Holy Spirit, but it was here in this poor, crumbling, forgotten ruin that he met God.

The church was probably quiet that day, as it is today. Unabashed, Francis slips down to the side of the altar and sits staring at the heaps of rubble and dust. He has been here before; he wonders why he has come again. Moments pass into hours, but still he sits, legs falling asleep beneath him. He has nowhere else to go but here. This is his home, he belongs here for some unknown reason.

Perhaps it is the solitude. With no one watching his comings and goings he can talk aloud or shout his questions and raise his fist in anger at his confusion and lack of direction. He can also sink down with tears burning his eyes and sob, "Who are you, Lord? Why do you draw me in, as if on a baited line? What could you want of me? I am no one, I don't even particularly care for your ceremony and tithes...yet, I love you."

The dam breaks and he stands before the crucifix trying to grasp the suspended wood to feel some comfort, some empathy from the painted, linear wounds. His tears reveal the gilded cross beneath its dust, but still it hangs lifeless and dumb. He pushes away, ready to leave, angrily thinking that he has cried out futilely again.

"Francis."

He stops frozen in his steps.

"Francis!" It is louder.

He knows that voice. He has heard it before in his dreams, at Spoleto. He turns and faces the cross, which now has pulse and depth. Life surges around him as the world echoes his name.

"Go and repair my Church, which as you see is falling to ruin around you."

He listens for more. It seems the universe held its breath for a moment, but now the voice is gone. He hears only the wind in the olive trees. The cross hangs lifeless again. He falls to his knees, weeping tears of joy and ecstasy. "Yes, my Lord." At last a sign! Direction and purpose! Not immediately recognizing the breadth of the command, Francis sets off to find rocks and mortar to rebuild San Damiano's walls.

Whatever he received in that sacred encounter was the precious impetus to holiness that has been given to so few, yet sought by so many. And as I walk back up the dusty road to Assisi I can see Francis, running and leaping half crazed, grabbing people's shoulders and twirling them around in a make-believe minuet of love. Love—that is what Francis met in San Damiano. And that is why he was able to skip lightly in glee rather than walk somberly away from such a weighty command.

Priest of San Damiano

During Francis' conversion he was moved to pack all he owned onto his horse, ride to Foligno and sell it all to give the money to the poor. Walking back, he passed by the old church of San Damiano, which was in desperate need of repair. He went inside, knelt and kissed the hands of the old priest who lived there and offered him the money. The priest tossed the coins out the window like so much sand, knowing full well who Francis was and the riotous life he led with his friends. Francis persisted earnestly until the priest finally agreed to take Francis in and teach him of God.

Little is recorded about the old priest who lived at San Damiano. I'm sure that Francis must have modeled a lot of his early life after him, whoever he was. I like to think that they were two kindred spirits, refugees camping in God's house. Sitting here in the courtyard, with swallows swooping and diving under the eaves, I wonder how many times Francis sat here and poured his heart out to this sympathetic, wise old man. I imagine their conversation:

"Come here, 'Ceco, sit with me and enjoy the peace of this evening."

And Francis answers, staring blankly at the sunset, "I can't enjoy it, Father. I saw my brother in the Piazza today. He made fun of me and threatened me about leaving my family. He says my father's anger grows with each day I am gone."

"So why worry and let it ruin this beautiful night?" Motioning one arm to Assisi and the other to the dry grass and stones around San Damiano, "They are there, and we are here."

And so Francis stays with the old priest. And as he looks at the priest's worn peasant face with its childlike eyes that laugh and dance in the moonlight, he wishes they could stay there forever with just the sky, their Lord and the night. But he wonders deep down inside if such precious things could ever be held onto and if one should even try.

A Secret Path

It is believed that Lady Pica was of French birth, brought to Assisi by her espoused Pietro who met her on a cloth-buying trip to France. At birth, Lady Pica named their son John, but Pietro later changed the child's name to Francis in honor of his wife's native land.

Lady Pica, how you must have loved your son. You understood his moods and were always there. Francis could never fail at anything in your eyes, even when he did not succeed. Francis was your heart's darling. You taught him French and the legends of the troubadours; you were his mentor and confidante and taught him of God. You were his mother. You could feel his restlessness and sense what he heard in the wind. For Francis could hear what others did not, and for that he suffered much.

How it must have broken your heart when your husband forbade Francis to return home after the scene before the bishop. Did you steal away at night when the mist lay damp and cool on the path to meet Francis and pray with him and show him your support? With the sky dark blue and bright with stars, as it is tonight, did you sit on some hidden step or walk a deserted garden path? Were your words muffled by the laughter echoing from bars through the city streets and cradled by soft chickens' cackling behind house walls?

Morning would find you both damp and cold, stiff from staying awake all night. Saying goodbye to your son and promising to meet him again on another night, you would go quickly, unseen, to your house and start the morning's work before Pietro discovered you had gone.

The Leper Hospital

In the Middle Ages almost every town had a leper hospital. Midway between Assisi and the Portiuncula the present-day Casa Gualdi stands on the site of the 13th-century San Salvatore delle Pareti leper hospital. According to legend, one day on the road Francis overcame himself and embraced a leper, and the stench of his sores were transformed into sweetness at this beginning of Francis' inner conversion to God

I've never seen a leper, let alone hundreds of these people in a leper colony. But this modern stuccoed villa with healthy green plants and shaded grasses was the once dilapidated leper hospital where Francis and his brothers came daily to minister.

Today the road is well-traveled and attractive. But in Francis' day, though it was a branch of the main thoroughfare from Rome to France, it passed through forest and marshland suitable only, it was thought, for lepers, criminals and other social outcasts. I wonder how often Francis heard the blood-chilling warning, "Unclean! Unclean!" And how often did he wince or run or hold his breath and turn his eyes away as an infected leper was led past him and his friends beyond the town walls into the wilds? Little did he know that one day he would choose to join them and learn from them the paradox of redemption.

What did he see in that first leper's eyes that drew him close? What did he recognize that drove him to embrace this "foul and repugnant" being? Perhaps he saw his own soul as he himself envisioned it: rotting, stinking, slowly being eaten away by an undesired, invisible evil, yet with a deep underlying stream of goodness, integrity and compassion. He saw and accepted the lepers' ugliness and deformity; but he also saw them as human beings, people created and loved by God. They stirred in his heart a memory of his own illness and rejection and released a great longing to help.

Francis considered himself the greatest sinner God could find. What better instrument to reveal God's redeeming power and healing love? So too with the lepers; their uncleanness became a living symbol of his own sinfulness. Here among their mats and bandages he would accept both the light and the darkness present in all human existence. Francis was slowly healed by the gratitude of the lepers as he mercifully washed away their loneliness and tended their sores. And the lepers breathed new life fresh with the Spirit of God and fragrant in the knowledge that they were purposeful and useful, able to give life in return for the comfort and concern given to them.

Francis used this place as a training

ground for those who would follow him. They too must recognize their true selves and accept their inner darkness, lest they be forever deceived into believing that because they had given their lives to God they were incapable of evil.

How wise you really were, Francis, to know that there is a leper in all of us that must be brought into the healing presence of God, to be tended to before we are transformed into life.

Road to Armenzano

*Caves were an important part of
Francis' life. During his conversion,
seeking guidance for his dreams and
visions, he would go to a cave whose
location is not known. Here he prayed
for long hours while an unnamed friend
patiently waited outside the cave's
mouth. Later, when the brothers joined
Francis, caves became a central part of
their existence. They sought shelter in
the crevices and outcroppings of the
Carceri and Mt. La Verna.*

Above the road to Armenzano there
is a little ridge which overlooks the north side of
Assisi. I love to come here to sit and rest. No
matter how still the air may be in the walled streets
of Assisi, here the breeze always rocks the weeds.
Even in the birds' chattering and squawking there is
an immense silence. And I am greatly surprised that
the silent woods are not unlike the rolling hills of
Pennsylvania that I climbed in my youth.

Somewhere outside Assisi's walls Francis
had a cave retreat. I don't really know why, but I've
often sensed it was here, near the back side of
Assisi where the quarry is. Cutting through the
limestone and clay, the torrent Tescio carves here a

perfect place for caves and solitude.

I'm glad that Francis sought peace and knowledge of God in nature. For what can be as still as the sky or as beautiful and complex as a mountain pasture? Francis was a very complex man, but somehow despite his complexity, his own nature was ultimately placid. And that is why Francis chose the mountain roads and caves when his soul longed for oneness with God.

Silence

It is
not so much
what you hear
in silence
as what you
let go
of.

Francis' Cave

Francis found something in his cave, something so profound and startling that his whole life was changed. Within him stirred a profound awareness of another presence. The presence came slowly at first, here and there, with anxious days in between wondering if it would ever return. It was as tangible as a solid wall, yet at the same time as elusive as the fog. It kept his heart waiting. Then one day it stayed and never left again.

Somewhere in the screaming and crying out of his failures and frustration Francis arrives at a cavern within himself. The damp, cool walls of the cave close in upon him. An overwhelming power envelopes his senses, funneling downward, flash-flooding his void with an inward rushing of itself.

Francis lies exhausted on the earthen floor. Opening his eyes slowly, aware that he is no longer alone, he raises himself and stumbles to the mouth of his cave. With one arm for support and the other raised against the brightness of the clear morning sun, he hears the Angelus rung from far-off San Pietro. His heart leaps with each strike of the clapper. He is changed, and he is frightened.

Walking back towards Assisi, he is aware that he is viewing a new world, his eyes trained for the first time on the magnificence and wonder around him. He breathes deeply; the cool air caresses his lungs and praise rises spontaneously to his lips. Tears rush to his eyes and he buries his head in his palms, realizing the presence is the very breath of life itself: God. And what was once mere countryside is now an enchanted garden.

Every day Francis returns to this cave. The empty darkness becomes the vessel of God's flowing love. And the channel of love between Francis and his Lord streams silent and deep, keeping nothing for itself, never swelling into a lake of pride. Daily the presence flows around and within him. The rock and coldness of his heart warm, supple in the hands of God.

Bernard's House

Bernard was the first companion of St. Francis. The stories tell us that after hearing Francis preach and witnessing Francis' spirit of prayer, Bernard gave up all his earthly possessions, distributed his money to the poor, and followed Francis.

Skipping lightly down the winding staircase of Via Buscatti towards the Piazza Vescovado, I notice a plaque resting on the upper story of a house. It bears the name of Bernard of Quintavalle. This was his family's home. Sitting back on the steps in the cool shade of a wall, I look up and study the house, imagining what it is like inside and who Bernard really was.

It was to this house that Francis came after his conversion. Thinking his friend to be asleep, he prayed throughout the night, "My God and my all," until falling exhausted onto his pallet at dawn. His prayer was not a plea, not an intercession, but a statement of purpose, an intimate call through the night.

But Bernard did not sleep. He stayed awake listening to his friend and discovered Francis' new love. And for many days and nights afterward Bernard listened. Only now Francis talked to him in excited outbursts and long pauses of joy and ecstasy.

Staring up at the plastered, regal house proud in the streaming sunlight, I see Bernard closing its door for the last time and walking down through the city gate towards San Damiano.

Now he would serve God. He had been wealthy and educated, a prime candidate for learning other languages and life-styles. Perhaps that is why he accompanied Francis to France and Spain.

He was at Francis' side when Sister Death took his friend. After Francis died, Bernard set about the task of keeping Francis' simplicity and poverty alive. He continued to live in caves, though the era of Brother Elias' monastery-building was at hand. He died in Assisi, faithful to the call he had heard from Francis' lips that long-ago night.

Bernard loved Francis and he loved God. He was the first to hear the dream and the first to join the brotherhood. He was Francis' friend, not just his follower. And in that distinction lies the purpose of his giving and the meaning of his love.

Walls

The Franciscans were to live as *fratelli,* brothers. They were to be a family with the blood of the Lord flowing between them and giving them life. They were not to strive for education or public recognition and were greatly discouraged from becoming hermits or secluding themselves from the others. They were to live among the common people without possessions or property, accountable and vulnerable to all. Francis wanted his brothers to be pilgrims in this life, desiring no other but their heavenly home. They were to be servant and field hand, healer and comforter whenever and wherever the need arose.

It is a very brave thing to be such a flagrant example, to allow total ridicule and objection to your beliefs. Giving up homes and businesses and donning peasants' tunics instead of silken hose is an extremely noticeable stand— especially in a small town like Assisi where nothing goes unnoticed. Perhaps that was the secret of the brotherhood's impact: They were so visible. Look at them—hungry, dirty, begging and praying in the streets, singing joyous thanks over crumbs of bread. They had no walls so there was no hiding. This above all taught humility.

This reliance on God also taught great freedom and trust, and brought great peace. Thousands came to the brothers for that peace. People could see their joy in their eyes and hear it on their lips, and they wanted to share it.

But not all the brothers found that freedom. Many became embittered and confused, seeking to blame circumstance for the failure in their own hearts to recognize and live their dream. Anger and judgment arose. Brother fought against brother, and what was once reality became only an ideal again. And the freedom of trust was lost as walls were built around every new analysis and interpretation.

Today the walls are as hard and striped as those hewn from Assisi's quarry. You don't hear the Angelus sung in the fields anymore and the enthusiasm of the brothers' voices seems stifled and far away behind expanses of forbidding stone and wooden gates.

I wonder what Francis would think of all the walls his followers have built to observe his way of life. He lived among the forests and the mountaintops, the lepers and the farmers' fields. I sense that "observers" are all we will ever be until we tear down the walls of our hearts and minds and let the Umbrian sun shine within us, so we won't be afraid anymore.

Rivotorto

In Francis' time Rivotorto was little more than a makeshift shelter near a brook. Francis and his earliest brothers, among them Bernard and Peter Catanii, settled here sometime in 1209 to live out their first rule of life. The place was so cramped and dilapidated that Francis wrote the name of each brother on the ceiling beam under which each would sleep and pray. The modern church is built near the site of the brothers' shed with a replica inside depicting a possible reconstruction of Francis' Rivotorto.

I'm walking down the path from San Damiano to Rivotorto. In front of me, a peasant is slapping the rump of his swine with a rod. I remember that Rivotorto was once a pigsty and that Francis and his brothers were once actually driven out of their shelter when an obstinate farmer prodded his donkey in among them.

I have often wondered why all of the first brothers are not canonized saints. They all lived the same rule, they all fasted as much as Francis. Many times, in fact, they did even more severe penances and had to be lovingly reminded that the Lord seeks mercy over sacrifice.

One brother nearly starved himself to death and cried out in the night, "I'm dying!" Francis had all the brothers get up and eat a bowl of broth with the starving brother so that he would not feel alone or chastised for doing what he thought was love. Other brothers put bands of iron around their bodies, and Francis warned them not to be so strict in their observance of penance.

If they all lived the same life-style, then it must be God's choice, not what we do, that makes the difference between saints and ordinary mortals. God chose Francis in a special way. God showed his approval in the stigmata, the ultimate sign of intimacy, the paradox of love and pain, togetherness and separation, the searing yet healing touch of love's fire.

It was God's love that was everything to Francis, not poverty or simplicity or humility. Because of it, Francis could be himself. God's love is forever and for all, and Francis knew that. He knew that nothing he could ever do would impress God. It is God who makes saints, not we.

Francis had only to be and to give himself. The rest was God's work. This is why Francis' very life became a prayer and why praise was spontaneously on his lips and why he could live happily in a pigsty. He could praise God in all things and in all situations because he had no expectations except to be as nothing. And that is why Francis was able to be consumed by the fire of love like a leaf lying naked on the ground, no longer clinging to any tree but willing to be placed in the hearth to yield itself freely to the flames.

fallen leaves

piles of leaves
on the ground
beneath each tree
unique
what has fallen
not as sweet
as how freely
bequeathed
each leaf

Portiuncula

*On the plain below Assisi stands the
Basilica of St. Mary of the Angels. It
was built in 1569 to protect the
"birthplace" of the Franciscan Order,
the Portiuncula ("little portion").
Francis and his brothers lived in mud
huts close to this beloved chapel.
Francis died here in 1226; a small
reliquary contains his bandages and
cord. Huge crowds of pilgrims flock to
this spot for a Plenary Indulgence given
on August 2, the anniversary of the
chapel's dedication.*

The giant basilica hovers over the tiny
church, like a mother protecting a frail child, shielding
it from wind and cold, literally putting herself between
it and any threatening adversary. Almost womb-like,
the basilica has nurtured the Portiuncula's life for
hundreds of years. Without the mothering basilica, the
little chapel would have crumbled away from exposure
to the elements or, perhaps worse, nakedness before
human schemes.

There is a holiness about this place,
perhaps because more than any other Franciscan
shrine or church it was part of the life and the
death of St. Francis. It is not hard to imagine that

this was the center of his dream.

As a young man Francis caught fish to pay the yearly rent of one basketful to the Benedictines. Here the brothers, with the forest close about them, sang their evening Compline; their praises echoed up the mountainside to the people inside Assisi's walls. Here their small cooking fires dotted the forest clearing, a witness to the city and travelers-by that the brothers' hearts were warmed and inflamed by the fire of love.

Here they were taught to beg and to cry and to laugh in ecstasy, and to share—painfully at times—the reality of their empty stomachs and aching limbs. And here is where Juniper joyously danced, throwing this and that into a grand fiasco of a soup to greet his brothers' return—but also to diminish their supplies and remind them of their call to simplicity and their commitment not to provide for the future.

It is this life and this spirit of Francis that flows from Santa Maria degli Angeli throughout all of Umbria, Italy and the world, giving new birth to Franciscans everywhere.

As I ride the bus back up to Assisi, the gold dome of the basilica flashes in the sun, reminding me of the richness of true poverty and the unmistakable brightness of a soul consumed by the love of God.

St. Francis and the Doves

Towards the rear of the Basilica of St. Mary of the Angels there is a corridor leading past the statue of St. Francis and the Doves through the rose garden to the brothers' huts. One night Francis was severely tempted, and wanting to chastise his body, walked into the cold winter's air and threw himself into the rosebushes. But the roses shed their thorns as they met with Francis' flesh. Today the thornless roses grow behind grilled arches, and specks of red on their leaves remind us of Francis' blood.

In the passageway behind the Portiuncula chapel is an unornamented statue of Francis standing above a languid pool of water. His hands are stretched outward, his palms cupped. The first time I walked by I noticed a pair of snow-white doves nestled in his open hands. At first I thought they were ceramic, but then one of them gazed downward curiously and, as if surprised by my surveillance, flew from the nest and perched on the saint's head. Later that night a priest told me that white doves have nested there for over 100 years; each generation hatching and taking first flight through the marbled halls of the basilica,

maneuvering safely through the thornless garden.

The pair I saw made me think of Benedict and Francis. Externally their Orders today seem as different as night and day. Benedictines prefer to be stationary and stable in their universities and monasteries. Franciscans still promote more of a wayfarer, knight-of-the-road attitude, though they too have their seminaries, universities and cloisters.

But surely Francis admired the dream of his brother Benedict. The great monk had been dead over 700 years, but his influence still dominated religious orders of the West during the time of St. Francis.

Francis sought solitude and prayer in the caves of Subasio as Benedict sought the mountain heights of Subiaco. Both were of wealthy heritage; Benedict's family could send him to be educated in Rome. Like Francis, Benedict was repulsed by human dealings and sought his companionship with God. Both underwent agonizing temptations of the flesh; both hurled themselves into briar patches to scourge themselves "clean." Both sought to remain aligned with the earth and the common people and insisted that their followers do arduous work with their hands.

Francis visited Benedictine hermitages. A monk at Mt. Subiaco painted the earliest known picture of him there; it still remains on the rock wall. It seems as if the Benedictines "nursed" the newly-born Franciscan tradition as it grew. They rented the brothers their beloved Portiuncula chapel; they took Clare in at the San Paolo and

San Angelo di Panzo convents till she moved to San Damiano.

Hundreds of years of rules and revisions, disagreements and disruptions have skewed both orders, especially as the pressures of the modern world crowd and crop the free-spirited wings of the true contemplative and the true pilgrim.

The dove returns from her cranial perch and I think of her chicks and to what heights they have flown. I am certain that they skirt the chiseled ledges of Subiaco as they do the sprawling farmland of the Umbrian plain.

Carceri

An hour's walk up Mt. Subasio is one of Francis' favorite hermitages, Eremo delle Carceri. Here Francis and his earliest brothers, Masseo, Rufino, Leo and Angelo, prayed in small mountain caves. Francis' cave was deep within the cliff and had a tiny altar at which Father Sylvester would celebrate Mass for the saint. After Francis' death, St. Bernardine of Siena built a hermitage here. Later it was enlarged and a chapel added. Nearby leans an ancient tree. Its branches were once crowded with birds who fell silent at Francis' invitation to hear God's Word. Franciscans have occupied the Carceri since Francis' time, preserving its solitude and starkness.

"Ready?"

"Yes."

"Want a sip of hot cocoa?"

"No, thanks. I just want to get started."

Out on the deserted streets, light gray with the sunrise, my two friends and I are hiking up to the Carceri. It is 5:30 a.m. and we hope to get there about seven, ahead of the tourists, and walk the paths and the forest in solitude as Francis did.

Rising up through the cool fog we finally round the last bend and can see the hermitage clutching Mt. Subasio's shoulder.

No one is here yet. The trees and the walls are ethereal in their netting of mist. The others want to pray morning prayer outside, much as the first brothers probably did. I leave them and slip down through the serpentine passage to Francis' cave.

Francis' cave! He slept here. He touched these very walls. How I wish they could tell me of all the things Francis did and said here, all the secrets that a bridegroom says only to his bride. Running my palm gently over their uncommonly warm surfaces, I can hear his cries of anguish and frustration over himself and his Lord. Here he tossed and turned in his bed feverish from fasting and abstinence. This rock held his firm, youthful body and slowly broke it down; as all flesh does, it slowly broke down and gave way to spirit. How sacred and privileged these walls to have heard him speak and sing in praise and love! They became to Francis what he had refused to possess: shelter, security and warmth.

My spell is broken by the footsteps and whispers of my friends, and I know this moment will soon be lost. Hurriedly, I bend down to hug the rock earth and kiss his sculptured bed. Suddenly, it becomes hard and cold like the substance it truly is.

Preaching to the Birds

Smooth
road of
flight
not
bound to
earth,
wisdom
of wings
that
soar and
skirt:
Politely
you
listen
to *my*
inspiring
word?
Oh,
teach me
of you
and what
you
have
heard.

Cave Dwellers

It's raining. I am outside Francis' cave waiting for the cloudburst to stop. How many times did Francis stand here at the mouth of his cave listening to the rumbling thunder? When the rain thudded on the earth and the forest floor surrounding his cave, Francis must have snuggled up inside the rock, safe and secure with his brothers close by and the love of his Lord in his ears, in his heart and on his lips.

When Francis lived, the earth was still considered the center of the universe. To the average person of his day the lightning and the thunder cracks must have seemed as if all God's wrath were focused on one spot. Perhaps that is why people were so obsessed with penitence and cleansing. They desired to be fresh and washed like the flower petals and trees, sparkling with God's love and mercy after the storm.

There was another man who lived in a cave and listened to the voices in the thunder. John the Baptist lived among the wild beasts when he came proclaiming a new age of repentance and glory to God.

Francis preached repentance, too. The example of his life and brotherhood heralded a new age for the Church, a deeper understanding of the "personalness" of God. And the corruption and darkness of Francis' time gave way to the glory of a Franciscan Renaissance just as the darkness of the

Old Testament gave way to the New.

Francis and John knew what it was to be born again from the womb of a cave in Umbria or the hills of Galilee. Their spirits were freed to cry the tears of a newborn child, to cling in total trust and love to the new-found arms which held them. And they grew up amidst all the storms and rumblings of earth with the certainty that their heavenly Father was surrounding them and protecting them forever.

As the rain puddles the entrance, I pull back into the mouth of the cave. I can hear the rushing torrent in the ravine and the slapping sheets of rain drenching the valley below. But the cave is warm and dry and I sit back, drawing my legs up tighter under me to wait and listen.

Wind

Silencing
me
in my
obedience
to
listen.

Lago Trasimeno

Lago Trasimeno is a shallow lake in the center of Italy where Francis came one year to spend the 40 days of Lent. The island grotto in which he stayed is now a small shrine; today a small town lies on the far side of the island. But no one was here when Francis came. It was wilderness.

Sometimes when I think of the saint in Francis, of all the miracles he performed and the hardships he bore, I forget that he had fears and failings too. I am at Lago Trasimeno today, where Francis spent 40 days alone. I know he did it to be in all things like his Lord, to experience the wild beasts and spirits of the desert. But when I think of the human, fearful side of Francis, I realize how vast the desert—the aloneness—must have seemed.

Francis must have feared the dark and being alone, for when he went to his caves he usually had a companion wait nearby. Once, in Rome at a cardinal's house, he became frightened of evil spirits and asked a brother to sit up with him. Maybe these fears came from his year of imprisonment in Perugia or from being locked in the cellar by his father. Either of these dark, damp, close dungeons could be quite traumatic for a high-spirited young man.

It is conceivable to me that Francis' long illness after his return from the war was some sort of "nervous breakdown." It is also possible that the evil in the world could not stand such an exceptional person and sought to destroy Francis through fear and harassment. Whatever the reasons, in that time of soul-searching he reached some profound answers that most do not reach until much later in life, if at all.

When he came to this island around 1210 he was older and knew the Lord, but he could also remember his past. At times in the night the reeds would move like as many phantoms swirling in the wind. Yet with each dawn the lake would lie in placid, misty beauty as stems of steam rose sparkling in the morning's rays. He found peace, shade and fragrance in the freshness of the morning woods, time to be alone and in love with his Lord. But the simple setting of the sun or the passing of a cloud cover could change the warmth and romance to cold and deception.

Slowly, with time, he befriended the howling winds and the rustling branches and stilled the waving reeds in the storms of his mind. He learned that it is only the things which we choose to accept that can be converted into life and wholeness, while those which we refuse to face blow around within us, empty as the wind but quite capable of destroying us.

As I sit on the rocks near the path to his cave, a sailboat with white sails billowing in the breeze is carried effortlessly through the water before me. And I wonder if sailboats would have tranquilized the horizon for Francis, too.

Ginestra

Choked by the dust and heat, ginestra clings tenaciously to the white rocky ground. For some reason this straggly but proud plant is a symbol to me of Assisi and all the legends and truths surrounding it. Similar in appearance to a forsythia bush, its trumpeting blossoms burst the otherwise parched landscape into a palette of bright acrylic yellow.

Did Francis love the plant too? I wonder if he rejoiced when its fragrance filled his lungs after a long journey away, or if the brothers ever used it to dress their drab caves and crumbling churches. I wonder if Francis ever presented Clare a freshly picked handful, saying, "Praised be you, my Lord, for Sister Ginestra, who is so tiny and frail but whose presence fills the whole room."

And sitting down to rest a minute near a country villa's gate, I breathe deeply the air filled with ginestra.

The Home of St. Clare

To the left of the Piazza San Rufino is the remaining wall of the original Favarone house. Clare was of noble birth. Her father, Count Favarone, is believed to have been the wealthiest man in Assisi. She was born in 1194, one of five children, and was baptized in San Rufino in the same font used for Francis 13 years earlier. Her name means "the bright and celebrated one," supposedly chosen by her mother, Ortolana, who received a message from God in prayer that the child would be a light for the whole world.

Clare, you are such a mystery. All morning I've been sitting here at the café across from your house, staring up at the windows, secretly hoping that a shutter would fling open and give me a glimpse of who you are. The Piazza San Rufino is speckled with darting bambinos kicking soccer balls. Teenagers try desperately to ignore their younger brothers and sisters, an air of independence and importance in their stance.

Francis no doubt stood here with his group of friends. They too probably teased and

laughed and conversed eloquently, trying to impress the townspeople with their new-found maturity and position. Years later he stood in another square alone, with no laughter, and laid his clothes at his father's feet, renouncing all his earthly possessions to follow his Father in heaven. You would have only been a little girl, maybe seven years old. But the scene left with you a deep, lasting impression and a longing to join this serious and mysterious young man.

Did you ever go back and visit your family after you ran away to join Francis? I know your sisters and later even your mother came to live with you at San Damiano. But what about your father? Did he approve or was he in sympathy with Francis' father, Pietro Bernardone? How hard it must have been to live in peace of soul and mind with such unresolved disruptions in your family life!

Most of your life can only be answered by more and more speculative questions. Who you really were and why is an unfinished puzzle. I have searched in your basilica and crypt, your cloister at San Damiano and now here at your house, hoping to find a continuous thread that will unravel your mysterious tapestry. But there is no single thread. There is only the braid of your love—of Francis, of God, of people.

But it was Francis' dream—his way of life, his suffering, his Lord—that gave your life meaning and substance. Maybe that is why you are considered a great contemplative and the very hearth of the Franciscan Order. The flame of your spirit burned not only for your own warmth but for

Francis and his dream. You were as a living sacrifice, an offering given freely for anyone to come to and benefit from the heat and warmth of a heart aflame with love of God.

And suddenly I see that you are not so much a mystery at all. For your story is told very clearly in the lives of all who love. It is not people who are the mystery but love itself. And the living of that love is as varied as the starkness of San Damiano, the intimacy of the Portiuncula, the richness of the Basilica of St. Francis. The sweetness of that love is as tender as Mary Magdalene, as worried and anxious as Martha, and as silent and constant as the Lord's mother Mary. Pondering, I understand a little better the selfless contemplative spirit and the great love that shaped the mystery you are.

Lady Mallard

smaller
willing to follow behind
her colors not as glamorous as
his
yet reminding everyone
of him

The Courtyard of San Damiano

The courtyard here at San Damiano is very tiny. Geraniums burst forth from their clay pots around the well, and the eaves and the overhangs of the outside walkway are dotted with swallows' nests. From here I can see Mt. Subasio and, down on the plain, to Rivotorto and the Portiuncula. Clare could see where Francis was, at least, even though she could not be with him.

All the journeys Clare made were in her heart. She could be in heaven with her Lord as easily as she could be with Francis in Rome. She had only to turn to the kingdom within her. Francis had taught her that on one of his preaching trips into Assisi before she entered San Damiano. He said that people could travel the world as pilgrims and own nothing yet have a home everywhere they went by entering into the cell within their heart. Francis carried his cell with him. Clare found her cell apart from Francis, in this secluded churchyard. She didn't need her cell for a home as Francis did; she always had walls and a roof, a refectory and a chapel. She needed her cell for love.

Although initially she may have followed Francis because she was infatuated with his dreams and talks of glory, once she and her sisters were alone at San Damiano Francis grew smaller, though never less cherished in her heart. When she was left alone with love, he who is love emerged. And Clare discovered a whole new world of love and presence in Jesus.

She could always turn to him, or frolic with him in the poppies or sit quietly with him long into the night. She could talk and ask his opinion, pray for people, be assured of Francis' safety and be comforted during the sadness of separation. Her Lord was always with her; in him a lifetime's worth of travel and excitement was wrapped up in daily meetings of deep contemplative prayer.

The room within her heart grew till all the brothers and the Poor Ladies, Francis and all the townspeople could fit into her once tiny cell, bursting its grill open as a soul content with listening love poured out its life and hope to the world. And a courtyard content with geraniums and swallows thrived from an inexhaustable well.

Well

Reach
down
farther still
and
bring
forth
within yourself
living
water,
whose
life
will nourish
and refresh
you
and
whose
birth
spills
forth the
seed
of
God.

La Verna

*About 90 miles northwest of Assisi in
the rugged region of Tuscany stands La
Verna. This secluded mountain was
given to Francis in 1213 by Count
Orlando, who had been greatly
impressed by Francis and offered this
hermitage in exchange for spiritual
counsel. In September, 1224, Francis
spent 40 days here in fast to prepare for
the feast of St. Michael. During this fast
a seraphic angel appeared to Francis
and united him forever with Christ
through the sacred stigmata. Today La
Verna is a place of pilgrimage. A
Franciscan hermitage there contains
many Della Robbia terra-cotta artworks
and chapels of other early Franciscan
saints such as Bonaventure and Anthony
of Padua.*

La Verna is the mountain that
Francis owned. As our taxi winds crazily up its
sides, I am secretly happy that Francis did own
something—and what a something, a whole
mountain! Speeding past some ruins on our right, I
am told they are the remains of Count Orlando's
castle. He admired Francis and his brothers and

wanted to give them a secluded and prayerful place for a hermitage: this wild and beautiful mountain.

It *is* prayerful here. With its deep and ancient forest, sheer cliffs and caves, the mountain is more inspiring and awesome than any basilica or shrine made by human hands. The others with me are hoping that the heavy morning mist lifts and the sun dries the water-bundled leaves and branches, but I pray otherwise. To me, the droplets on the darkened trees and the quiet steaming boughs are ethereal and alluring. Walking up the steep path to the pinnacle, climbing granite boulders, and pausing to lean against a giant fir tree, I feel Francis in the heaviness of the mist, draping his mantle of love around me.

So often when I think of him and his austere poverty, I forget that he and his brothers really did have many things, from kitchen pots and pans to tables to La Verna. His wealth far surpassed his poverty on this mountain. And it is not surprising to me that here at the summit of the paradox of rags become riches, the Lord would once again enflesh himself in the poorest of the poor.

The mist never did clear. The taxi on the way home is cold and damp. My clothes and shoes are wet from the forest floor, but my heart is warm and happy. Glancing back at the darkened mound of fog I know we too have shared in God's revelation and will forever possess a share of La Verna and of what happened there.

Gubbio

Soon after Francis' conversion, he was attacked by robbers on the road. After recovering a few days at a nearby monastery, he went to visit a friend in Gubbio, a small town approximately 20 miles north of Assisi. This friend gave Francis his first hermit's tunic. Francis revisited Gubbio often, performing many miracles and cures. The most famous legend is about a dangerous wolf who terrorized the citizens and the livestock. In 1220 Francis tamed the wolf and the animal became protector of the city. Today the church of San Francesco della Pace is located where the wolf lived and is thought to be buried.

The people with whom I'm staying have a dog named Lupeta, "little wolf." One very hot day as I was taking her for a walk, the normally frisky shepherd got weaker and weaker, her tongue dangling to one side of her slobbering jaw. I reached down to try and comfort her, assuring her that we would be home soon. As I gave her some of my water and stroked her head, Lupeta raised her eyes. For an instant I thought I saw myself there, looking gratefully upward. I thought of Francis and the wolf of Gubbio and wondered if, when he looked into its eyes, he saw his reflection too.

Like the wolf, Francis had known rejection. He too had done incredible things to insure his own survival, such as stripping naked in a town square full of wide-eyed people. Surely the wolf had felt as much loneliness and sadness in being an outcast as Francis had.

When Francis walked up to the wolf, the half-crazed wild beast sat curiously still, staring at this little man approaching him. The two paused, wolf and man, and no one knew the thoughts they shared. Only they knew that they were really one and the same, separated merely by physical appearance. Each knew he must bravely tame something of the other within his own nature. The wolf gave Francis its paw and gently nudged its warm muzzle into his hands, and in the union of their understanding their fears faded away.

Francis confronted the wolf on its own ground and accepted the animal as a creature created for good, not evil. The wolf, in turn, sensing Francis' sincerity and harmlessness, received him in total trust. Francis and the wolf walked into Gubbio together and the people who had been staring in disbelief cleared a path before them. The once hated, feared wolf became friend and guardian to Gubbio. And Francis, singing the praises of creation's wholeness, galloped back to Assisi on his imaginary steed, feinting at ginestra bushes in his passing.

The Ivory Horn

*In June, 1219, Francis and a companion
sailed to Damietta, Syria, from Ancona,
Italy. The Crusades were raging in the
East; Francis sought to become one of
the sacred martyrs. In the fall of 1220,
Francis visited the Saracen camp to talk
to the Sultan of Egypt, hoping to
convert him to belief in Jesus. The
Sultan listened to Francis and saw he
was a holy and sincere man; for this
reason he let Francis go from the camp
unharmed. The Sultan gave Francis an
ivory horn, now displayed in the basilica,
to ensure his safe passage back to Italy.*

Francis, what did you hear in the
lapping waves? On your travels to the Holy Land
did you sit on the deck to watch and to listen?

Constancy, that is the rolling sea: always
coming, always giving—sometimes in moments of
wrath but then, with anger quickly past, a gentle
motion like a mother rocking her child to sleep.

I can hear Francis explaining parables
to Leo (for a good story is the way Franciscans
teach), telling how Jesus beckoned Peter to walk on
the waves—not on the water but on the turbulent
waves:

"Jesus said, 'Walk, Peter! Have faith!'

"In what? In the water, in Peter? No, in God's love! For you see, Leo, Jesus wanted Peter to know that waves are a part of everyone's life. But they can become as hard as stepping-stones, too, when you walk in faith and believe in them as part of God's plan for you."

Jumping up and running to the ship's rail, Francis and Leo skim stones that ride out into the sun-topped crests, wanting to dive in after them and give themselves up to sun and wind and sea.

Fonte Colombo

South of Assisi in the Rieti Valley is another hermitage, Fonte Colombo (Dove Spring). Here in 1223 Francis composed the second Rule for the Order. On the wall of the chapel a tau cross, a Greek T, *was painted by Francis' own hand. The* tau *echoes Ezekiel 9:4-6, which tells how those in the city of Jerusalem who were to be spared God's punishment were marked with a cross. The* tau *mark was seen on Francis' head by Brother Pacificus and became a major symbol of the Franciscan Order. In 1225 Francis had his infected eyes cauterized here, asking "Brother Fire" not to hurt him; the red-hot iron seared his flesh but miraculously spared him any pain.*

What is it about water that Francis loved so much? Maybe it drenched his parched soul, or he felt its beauty and strength as a presence of God on earth. Perhaps he would sit for hours, eyes closed and head raised, feeling the water seeping through him, washing away his sins and sufferings and refreshing him from within. Surely after being in the hot, enclosed towns or working with the lepers or sweating in the fields, he would come to this spring and rush to the water's edge, throwing handfuls of water in the air like a little child.

You can hear water long before you see it. Perhaps after a long trip away, its subtle trickle sent an urgency through Francis' body and he would kneel at the stream's edge, diseased eyes tearing, his soul ready to burst apart with longing to fling itself into the pool and glide away free to mingle and linger with God's touch on every rock and stone.

Whatever Francis felt about water, he returned to it often. Each time was a time of healing for him, whether he was deafened by the tumultuous white water sliding downward at the hermitage of Celle de Cortona or soothed by the forest springs here at Fonte Colombo, the Carceri and La Verna. Long before his conversion nature had soothed his spirit. And after the voice at San Damiano spoke, nature became more and more alive to him as he began to draw deep insights from sun and moon, water and earth. He longed to hear this voice again and again; perhaps he heard it in the whisperings of the water's flow.

Francis' constant return to water is like a child's returning to a treasured gift that his father made years before. He touches it as reverently and as lovingly as he did when he first received it. And each return deepened their pool as Father touched son and son embraced Father till a roaring river of love flowed between them.

Sister Water

You are so pure and chaste. You move
silently over everything you touch,
slowly and gently smoothing away all
roughness with your presence. You are
precious and do not waste yourself and,
after being given, return to the heavens
from where you came. The sound of
your returning brings tranquility and life
to all the earth. Therefore, shed your
tears upon me and teach me to love as
patiently and as purely as you.

Brother Fire

Upward sweeps
of inward rushing
fan your
smoldering soul
to flame.

Logs lie
upon your altar
of embered prayer
and ashen
gray...

Greccio

Greccio is a small mountain hermitage in the Rieti Valley between Assisi and Rome. The cliff on which it stands was made available to the friars by John Vellita. On the eve of December 25, 1223, Francis and the brothers and many laypeople from the nearby farms celebrated Christ's birth with real animals in a cave on this mountain. The infant Jesus appeared in Francis' arms to all those watching. Thus the tradition of the Christmas crib as we know it today began.

christmas eve

all is quiet
torches line the path
pilgrims come to do homage
snow falls to the ground
carols rise to fill the air
and oxen stand aside

as cave and spirit
bear a son

Return to La Verna

On this mountain, in a cave no more than a slithering crack in the earth, Francis received the stigmata. That is usually how we think of La Verna now, but what was it like before? What prayers did Francis utter here at sunset with the birds quiet and the mosquitoes swarming? Why was he drawn here? What was so special that of all places he should receive the stigmata here?

How often we return to the Lord in a special place, a favorite chair or pew in church. So it was with Francis. He would climb up here into his Father's lap, close to the very heartbeat of his life. Each time he would feel stronger, more assured of his Father's faithfulness and love. And Francis grew.

Usually, he was not even aware that he had grown. Only later would some circumstance recall a thought or lesson learned from the wind on a faraway mountain called La Verna. In his mind, no matter where he was, he could always return to the strength of this place. And because of this intimacy his spirit could soar to the heavens of Tuscany and mingle with the evening's drafts to float on God's invisible touch like a lark sailing on the wind.

St. Clare's Garden

*On the second story of San Damiano
there is a small opening leading from
the inside stairway through the wall out
onto a small, secluded balcony called
the Garden of St. Clare. During his
illness in the spring of 1225, Francis
came to San Damiano to rest and be
cared for by Clare and the Poor Ladies.
In his suffering he composed the
Canticle of Brother Sun, a song of
praise to all God's creation. Francis may
have been carried on a litter to be
warmed by the sun on this balcony, or
he may have composed the Canticle in a
make-shift hut beside San Damiano's
walls. A bronze plaque on the balcony
wall commemorates the traditional site
of the Canticle's composition.*

The space where Francis wrote the
Canticle of Brother Sun is so small. I have to duck
through a little opening in the wall to get to it; once
inside I find it only measures about five by eight
feet. Red geraniums decorate it and Brother Sun
bathes them with his love; they seem to grow very
well. It is bright and sunny in this niche. Other

legends say Francis wrote the Canticle in the darkness of a little twig hut that Clare had made for him outside her cloister walls.

The Canticle is a symbol of total integration between creature and Creator, like a fish in the sea and the sea in the fish. Francis saw all things touched by the hand of God and addressed them as brothers and sisters.

All of creation was united through the presence of the Holy Trinity, which became to him the banner of his heavenly family's heritage and the noblest of all coats-of-arms. Francis knew the secret of such unity. To be united was to be constantly and consciously present to the other as Francis was to his Lord and the Lord is to all creation. Francis' love of the Trinity was always on his lips, in his heart and in his mind. He began all his prayers with its praise and sought its unity and perfection in all that he did. That meant to be as uncomplicated as a circle but as integrated as a spiral.

To Francis creation was the outreach of the spiral from and through his Lord. Every creature became sacred because it flowed from God. God gave Francis the sensitivity to realize this fact to the point of feeling total oneness with something as tenuous as the wind. Water and fire, wind and earth became his home and family. And all living creatures became his brothers and sisters.

In this knowledge he became totally free to live as a beggar or talk to a wolf or a bird, to sing to a poppy or embrace a leper, to call God his own Father and to stand naked in the streets. For Francis knew he was at home with all creation and all creation knew it was at home with St. Francis.

Return to Portiuncula

What sadder sight could there be than Francis sprawled here on the ground, his cauterized eyes struggling to identify the outlines of so many brothers around him? The floor mat he lay upon and the frescoes depicting his passing are the visible reminders of his death, but they are sterile mementos of the real *Transitus*.

All of Francis' love and suffering met its fullfillment, as the long, seemingly eternal courtship finally erupted in a rush of passion and joy. The Beloved's touch, the out-rushing stream of freedom and release—what joy! What peace! At last his spirit was free to fly with the larks, to swoop and sing and sail through Assisi's streets reviving anyone who stops to breathe in its life.

Transitus

Brother Leo,
my robe I leave with you;
your laughter I take with me.
You are here.
I can not see you
but my heart knows
which tears are yours.

Climb, my little lamb,
over all the mountaintops
you can find
and bleat the joys
of purity and simplicity.

Remember that it is trust
that makes us grow
and it is love
which carries us
from mountain peak to mountain peak
to the Lover who meets us
in the whiteness of the
quieting snow.

St. Francis' Basilica

*Francis died on the eve of October 4,
1226, at the Portiuncula. The building
of his basilica was initiated by Brother
Elias (whom Francis named Vicar of the
Order) under the direct order of Pope
Gregory IX to raise a triumphant
structure to glorify the gospel poverty of
St. Francis of Assisi. On May 25, 1230,
Brother Elias placed Francis' body in a
secret crypt to ensure that no one would
steal the saint's remains. The basilica is
a treasure of paintings, frescoes and
mosaics, the most famous artists being
Giotto, Lorenzetti and Cimabue. The
plan of the church is a double T (the tau
symbol), an upper and lower church;
underneath is the crypt where St.
Francis is buried.*

Tonight the Swedish National Choir
is singing in the lower church. Voices like angels'
echo through the alcoves and filter here into the
courtyard. I sit on a wall, propped up against a
pillar just above the cistern. Here I can see the sky
and stars and breathe the cool mountain air. The
pink granite has not yet cooled from the day's sun;
its warmth seems alive and comforting. Although

this basilica is truly an architectural fortress, the pink and white stone, the Gothic arches and bells give it a light and airy atmosphere.

In your day, Francis, this was a potters' field where dead criminals and the poor whose families could not afford burial were thrown over the city wall to waste away in the sun. It was here that you wished to be buried among the people whom you loved. I wish they had left it at that, with maybe just a small cross, like the one you carried when you preached, marking your grave. Then in death as in life you would be truly little and poor.

But I don't blame Brother Elias for agreeing to build this basilica. He was trying to do what he thought was best to protect your body, more precious to him than his own life or reputation in the Order and in the Church. He hid your body so the rival towns of Perugia and Rome wouldn't try to steal you away or strew your relics all over Italy.

You loved Elias and at your death entrusted him with your dream and the brotherhood—with your life. I've heard awful things about Elias: how he persecuted your first companions for adhering to gospel poverty. He died outside the Order alone and forgotten. That doesn't surprise me. For the turmoil over the meaning of true poverty and the gospel life had already started before you died and continues to this day. Brothers fought against brothers; they even fought against you. Why would they not fight against Elias?

Elias and your first and most faithful

companions became "old and silly men,"
disregarded by the new brothers who came seeking
a saint rather than God. Perhaps it was good you
died when you did, Francis.

The Crypt

*Brother Elias did indeed merge Francis'
remains with the earth as Francis had
wanted. The exact location of the tomb
was unknown until 1818, when Pope
Pius VII ordered a third attempt to
locate and identify the sarcophagus. On
September 5, 1820, a body was located
and identified by the still present marks
of the stigmata. A crypt was built in the
neoclassic style but was thought too
ornate for the simple Franciscan
tradition and too different from the rest
of the basilica. In 1932 Ugo Tarchi, an
Assisian architect, completed the crypt
as we see it today: stark, moving,
Romanesque. Buried with Francis are
his earliest companions: Angelo, Leo,
Rufino and Masseo. Opposite Francis'
sarcophagus are the remains of Blessed
Jacoba dei Settesoli.*

Near the Circus Maximus in Rome,
half-hidden among the bushy plants, is a single
tower. According to legend, it is the remains of
Lady Jacoba dei Settesoli's estate. Her last name
means "seven suns," so I envision her as a woman
who brought great radiance and joy wherever she

went. She was a wealthy Roman matron, probably close to Francis in age. Her family owned large tracts of land in the Trastevere section of Rome. Somewhere near this tower Francis used to stop and eat a special sweetmeat prepared for him. To Francis she was more than a friend; she was *Brother* Jacoba.

As he lay dying, it was she for whom he asked; she was the only woman allowed into the cloister. She knew through a dream that Francis needed her at his side. As if to immortalize his request, she later sold her estate in Rome and came to Assisi to work and live among the poor for the rest of her life. Upon her death the brothers placed her remains in the hill with Francis, a silent statement of who you are, Fra Jacoba.

You were a woman whom Francis did not try to avoid in fear of being unfaithful to his Lord. Surely you were among the chastest of all women for Francis to feel he could be totally himself with you. You were mature enough not to be infatuated with this famous beggar and therefore could support him as only the most intimate friends can.

Your grave is relatively unknown compared to Assisi's other relics, and your poor brown metal box is passed unnoticed by most pilgrims. But I am thoroughly delighted that you are here, and that your grave is so humble and little. Francis would have wanted it that way.

The Vaults of Paradise

*Above the high altar in the lower church
are the four Vaults of Paradise,
generally believed to have been done by
Giotto. This group of frescoes decorates
the ceiling of the room directly above
Francis' tomb and was intended by the
early friars to be the most splendid work
in the basilica. Three of the triangular
frescoes show the vows of poverty,
chastity and obedience. The fourth
shows Francis in glory, surrounded by
angels and dressed in a rich dalmatic
robe.*

Lady Poverty, who were you in
Francis' heart? What allurements did you whisper
into his ear on a moonlit night? And what
fragrances did you raise up from the earth to draw
him so near?

I am standing in the lower church.
Above me are the four vaults of the sanctuary, the
famous Vaults of Paradise. In the allegory of Holy
Poverty, Lady Poverty is the bride and Francis the
groom. She has thorn bushes at her feet; their
straggly stems wind up and around her body and
blossom into delicate roses at her head. Jesus stands
between them, giving Francis her hand like a proud

father giving his most cherished daughter away.

Woman and symbol, bride and dream—to Francis poverty was the most beautiful, worthy lady any knight ever fought for. Her battlegrounds, the leper colony and the muddied streets, were more noble to him than the field of battle. The mud of Rivotorto and the cold, penetrating dampness of mountain caves became the silken tents of the most pompous tournament. Francis sang her love songs in the night and searched for joy and comfort in her bosom. She was his lady.

Lady Poverty

Briars
to
blossoms,
burdens
to
blessings
brought
by the
baring
of a
bride's
virgin
breast.

Betrothed
and
bequested
to
become
and
be tested
in the
heart
and the
loins
of the
groom's
burning
flesh.

Street Music

Tonight while walking down a side street towards the Basilica of St. Francis, I see an old *Schwester,* or German nun, playing her handmade guitar. An old man with drab, baggy pants and a cap is shuffling on the sidewalk next to her. Each is enjoying and appreciating the other and possibly remembering the old country. Both their eyes catch mine, but they are in no way embarassed though neither the dancing nor the playing is that good. Her picking follows me down to the basilica. With joy, I remember the lutes and zithers of Francis' time.

One story comes to mind. Francis was severely oppressed and wanted one of the brothers to get a zither and play for him to lighten his heart. The brother refused, saying he preferred not to indulge in anything so worldly. Francis explained to the brother that the saints played such instruments for the praise and glory of God and it was only the human evil of using them for sinful pleasures that made them worldly. But still the brother would not oblige Francis.

During the night, as Francis lay on his mat, a lutist was heard outside his window playing the tune that Francis had requested of the brother. No one could see the troubadour, as if an angel had come to play for Francis.

I am happy to know that Francis never gave up so much of the world that he forgot music.

Even his psalms and canticles were meant to be sung by the brothers, not merely spoken. Francis loved music, and it brought a deep inner peace to his body and spirit. He would sometimes twirl across the countryside, playing an imagined violin for any bird or tree he could find. He was able to hear a melody in every groaning of creation, in the suffering and the abandoned as well as the handsome and the beautiful. All externals became as nothing to him because he only heard the song of the Spirit living within every created being.

The songs Francis heard are still in Assisi, in the side streets and in the churches; but like every good piece of music, they must be listened to and appreciated for what they are, not for what they are not. Each person's interpretation will be unique, but every performance of the piece, expertly done or not, will bring great joy to the composer and the Creator. That is why Francis fiddled an imaginary violin and heard beautiful masterpieces from the poppy fields—and why the *Schwester* saw a perfect polka and the shuffling old man heard a perfect tune.

Francis

His love of God
was everything.
Therefore, his
poverty was
as nothing
because
he already
possessed
what was
all.

Assisi's Art

There is so much art in Assisi: Cimabue, Giotto, Lorenzetti; frescoes, fountains, and architecture. I've looked on tile after tile, into the eyes of statues and paintings waiting for life. It is the job of the artist—whether realist or impressionist, master or pupil—to capture and convey the truest meaning of any scene. The relationship between finished work and viewer is one of transformation. What is innate stirs emotion or thought as plaster wings seemingly soar and oil petals tantalize and invite the touch. But when human touch is met with canvas, the moment is lost. One beach can be captured but never a whole sea.

I don't know if Francis ever sculpted or drew. I only know he was the greatest artist of them all because his very life was art. He transformed all he experienced in prayer into a way of life. He communicated and conveyed everything he saw and said into hope, joy and love. His life was one continuous seascape with waves that rolled and rolled up from the ocean depths to exhaust themselves upon the sand.

The Cloister Orchard

Next to St. Clare's Basilica there is a low wall that borders the piazza and overlooks the cloister's orchards. As I take a seat on it this afternoon, I see an old peasant tanned and sweaty, cutting the weeds around the olive trees with a hand scythe. So often the frescoes that we see paint a very clean, pious picture, and we tend to forget that Francis and his brothers worked as common laborers, their bodies dirtied and their feet and hands caked with mud.

In the old man Francis suddenly becomes present for me, laughing and humming to himself about his Lord, his rough woolen habit pulled off his shoulders and draped from the rope cord hanging round his waist. Weeds and sod bury his feet. Young and recovered from years of sickness, I'm sure Francis, in a very human way, was proud of his body at work, alive and strong.

Francis loved the earth. To him it was as rich as all the tapestries that hung on the walls of the finest courts. His Lord had given him the earth as protection, womb and sustenance. The soil drew him close and there he could rest as in his mother's arms. In its coolness he found solace, in the darkness a listening presence and in the brightness of the day penetrating truth of the path he had chosen to follow.

But as the old man slowly straightens up, the light in the eyes I thought were Francis' is

filmed by years of unfulfillment and mediocrity. And the old man gazes around and then slumps back to his work, shrouded by his dissatisfaction, unaware that anyone else is even here.

Assisi Sun, Assisi Moon

This evening I watched the setting of the sun. The moon was already rising in the sky as the last flashes of warmth and brilliance yielded to the coming night. I thought of the movie *Brother Sun, Sister Moon,* and I thought of Francis and Clare of Assisi and how their lives followed the natural rhythms of nature.

Clare could never be Francis, just as the moon can never be the sun and the sun can never be the moon. The sun is huge, billions of times larger, encompassing many, many moons. Its power and light is generated deep within the molten viscera of its being. And with its magnetism it draws and leads an entire solar system of followers.

But in the evening as the sun sets, the darkness, which must follow after the light, appears. As the horizon darkens, Sister Moon steadfastly rises, faithful witness to the presence of Brother Sun. And west will follow east until rising again.

St. Clare's Basilica

Clare died at San Damiano in 1253 with her sisters and Brothers Juniper and Leo at her side. Her body was brought from San Damiano to the Church of San Giorgio, where Francis' body was also kept until the erection of his basilica. The Basilica of St. Clare was constructed on the exact site of the Church of San Giorgio in 1257-60. The Romanesque-Gothic church was designed by Filippo di Campello. Like Francis', Clare's body rested in an unknown location beneath the church until the 19th century. Today it is preserved in a crystal casket in the crypt. Off the main nave of the basilica is a room which holds the crucifix which spoke to Francis in San Damiano.

No one knows whether or not the crucifix spoke to Francis audibly. But I don't think it really matters, for it moved him much more than any word or whisper. It is a strange crucifix. It has such life, as if it truly could speak. From the moment you step inside the chamber its eyes are upon you; you can feel them everywhere in the room.

The crucifix hangs in a glass-covered case now, on a lime green velvet background. A light perpetually shines upon it. It leaves me wordless. Mere words could never capture what it communicates so loudly through the stillness. The corpus is frail. Hand-painted figures extend open palms to catch the flowing blood from Christ's hands and side and feet. But his face is serene. Almost totally indifferent to his state, he seems oblivious to all things except the person who is standing before him. His eyes do not look down in defeat nor pleadingly upward to God, but straight ahead, penetrating every other eye that meets his. He looks as if he is just ready to speak some profound secret, but he waits for me to speak first.

The artist, like Da Vinci, has captured the quizzical moment. To Francis, the lips parted and the moment spoke. And to all others who come here and sit in its presence another moment speaks, for someday all people must answer the question revealed—if only in speechless wonder and long searching glances held in the filtering of the light's burning rays.

Perfect Joy

The joy of poverty
is not to have nothing
in this world;

the joy of poverty
is to have nothing
but God.

Epilogue

I am a lay Franciscan. I've often wondered what that really means and what Francis had in mind when he initiated the "Brothers and Sisters of Penance," a "third order" which today is known as the Secular Franciscan Order. Two other lay Franciscans are here with me in Assisi; to me they are the people closest to what I think Francis intended.

Margaret brought all her articles for a two-month stay in a Pan-Am shoulder tote. All of her clothing is brown. She wears closed-heel-and-toe sandals, even through the winters of Boston, and a Franciscan cross around her neck. At home she works for her room and board, owning nothing but a secondhand moped.

Marilyn's appearance is much the same as Margaret's, but she is a university professor from Jerusalem. Their backgrounds are so different but their goal is the same: to love God with their whole heart in detachment from worldly opinions or standards and to give witness to their Franciscan vocation in all things.

Thomas of Celano tells us that hundreds of such people were running to join Francis in the early days of the Order. To accommodate their wishes without disrupting their previous commitments to Church and family, Francis established the "Brothers and Sisters of Penance."

The thrust of Francis' preaching is "becoming." Pray, fast, beg, preach, work, be joyful—these are all exhortations to action. The Penitents were to strive to "become" in the world as perfectly and as wholly as the brothers and Poor Ladies who had "left" the world. Since no one can truly leave the world as long as they are alive, the issue becomes how heart and talents can best respond to the Lord as we perceive him around us.

And now, when I see a pair of closed-heel-and-toe sandals in the marketplace or a store window, I think of Margaret and Marilyn and then I think of Francis. My heart is certain that I'm following the right footsteps. And my spirit looks forward to skipping and, maybe later, to running.

What Was Mine to Do...

The dying Francis said to his brothers:
"I have done what was mine to do;
may Christ teach you what you are to do."
2 Celano 214.

Walk, pilgrim,
walk,
searching
for what you thought
you had
but now can no longer
find,

what you believed
would companion you
only to discover
that it brought
and left you
at the forest's edge.

In you must go
alone
with only
memory
to guide you
and to recognize
me,
should we meet
again.

The Life of St. Francis: A Chronology

1181: Francis is born in Assisi.

1193: St. Clare is born.

1202 (November): Perugia and Assisi are at war.
Francis begins a year-long imprisonment in Perugia.

1204: Francis suffers a long illness.

1204 or early 1205: Francis receives a vision and a
message in Spoleto; his conversion begins.

1205 (fall): Sam Damiano crucifix speaks to Francis.

1206 (early): Francis' father takes him before the bishop.

1206 (spring): Francis nurses lepers in Gubbio.

1206 (summer and fall): Francis returns to Assisi and
begins repairs on San Damiano.

1208 (April 16): Brother Bernard, Peter Catanii and
Brother Giles join Francis at the Portiuncula.

1208 (summer): Four more brothers join.

1209 (spring): Francis goes to Rome with 11
companions. Pope Innocent III approves his brief
Rule. The brothers settle first at Orte and then
at Rivotorto on their return to Assisi.

1209 or 1210: The brothers move to the Portiuncula.
Possibly the beginning of the Secular Franciscans
(Third Order).

1211 (spring): Francis spends Lent at Lake Trasimeno.

1212 (March 18/19): Clare is received at the Portiuncula.

1212 (May): Clare moves from the Benedictine
convent to San Damiano.

1213 (May 8): Count Orlando offers Francis Mount
La Verna.

1213 thru 1215: Francis and his brothers continue
their missionary trips. Francis goes to Spain.

1216 (July 16): Pope Innocent III dies. Honorius III
is elected his successor.

1216 (summer): Portiuncula indulgence is obtained from Honorius III.

1219 (May): First Franciscan missionaries leave for Morocco. Francis sails to Damietta.

1219 (fall): Francis visits the Sultan.

1220: The first Franciscan martyrs are killed in Morocco; Francis goes to the Holy Land.

1220 (summer): Francis returns to Italy.

1220: Peter Catanii is named vicar when Francis resigns.

1221 (spring): Peter Catanii dies. Elias is named vicar.

1221: Rule of Third Order is approved by Honorius.

1223: Francis composes the Second Rule of Fonte Colombo; it is approved in November.

1223 (December): Francis sets up the first Christmas crib for Mass at Greccio.

1224 (August 15 - September 29): Francis fasts at La Verna; receives the stigmata in September, probably the 14th.

1225 (early): Francis stays in a hut at San Damiano while St. Clare cares for him in his sickness.

1225 (April or May): Francis composes the Canticle of the Sun. His eyes worsen.

1225 (July): Urged by Elias and Cardinal Hugolin, Francis goes to Fonte Colombo to have his eyes cauterized.

1225 (late summer): Francis receives more treatment to his eyes and ears.

1226 (August - early September): Francis is taken to the bishop's palace in Assisi, his health failing.

1226 (September): Realizing he will die soon, Francis insists on being carried to the Portiuncula. He blesses the city of Assisi.

1226 (October 3): Francis dies at the Portiuncula.

1226 (October 4): Francis is buried at San Giorgio Church.

1228 (July 16): Gregory IX canonizes St. Francis.

1253 (August 11): St. Clare dies at San Damiano.